Under Glass

poems by

Mary F. Lachman

Finishing Line Press
Georgetown, Kentucky

Under Glass

ACKNOWLEDGMENTS

Much gratitude goes to James Scaramuzzino, Jennifer Iszkiewicz, and
Carolyn Nemec who read my drafts and made suggestions on everything
from word choice to organization.

Many thanks to the nurses, doctors and support staff who cared for me and
continue to follow me.

Special thanks to my dear friends, Maureen Zakowski and Carolyn Nemec,
who were two of the few people with whom I shared my deepest thoughts
and concerns.

And finally, my love and gratitude to Dominick Scaramuzzino, who knew
the depth of this journey as his own.

Publisher: Leah Maines
Editor: Christen Kincaid
Cover Art: Michael Scaramuzzino
Author Photo: Dominick Scaramuzzino
Cover Design: Elizabeth Maines McCleavy

Author inquiries and mail orders:
Finishing Line Press
P. O. Box 1626
Georgetown, Kentucky 40324
U. S. A.

Table of Contents

The Club 1

Flip a Coin 2

Destiny 3

I Bend at the Garden 4

Physiology Experiment 5

Tail between My Legs 6

Stranded 7

Friend 8

Risk Factor 9

Silence 10

Walk with Me 11

Chemo-smiles 12

Solo Trip 13

Don't Ask 14

Drowning 15

Swimming 16

Markers 17

Battleground 18

New Things I 19

New Things II 20

New Things III 21

New Things IV 22

August 8th 23

Time Passes 24

Good Will 25

All in the Art 26

On Paper 27

Holiday Letter 28

2yr 2mo 12d 29

Epilogue 30

To my family

The Sailor cannot see the North
But knows the Needle can.

~Emily Dickinson in a letter to
Thomas Wentworth Higginson, 1862

The Club

I didn't want to join the club
not now or ever
but still I thought it might be in the cards
like the pilot in a plane crash
or the captain in the shipwreck
because I am a pathologist.
This is what I do.
I diagnose disease.
I look at little pieces of people under glass,
the human body seen under the microscope:
bacteria, viruses, bumps and cancer.
I tell the other doctor what is wrong
so why shouldn't I be under glass too?

Flip a Coin

I wish I could be the woman under the glass today.
She is 67. I am 58. She is
ten years older, but
her breast biopsy is normal.
I know we shared the anxiety
of being told about a blip in the shadow
of the mammogram
and the biopsy that followed
from the blade in the surgeon's hand.
And then a moment of not knowing
the hours of waiting.
The outcome and your future
hangs in the air,
like a coin
tossed in the air at the start of a game
to see which team will kick off and
which will receive.
You wait
patient or not.
You wait for the coin to drop.
Heads up or
tails down.
Hers landed up.

Destiny

It hits you when you aren't looking.
It tosses rocks in your path
and changes your life in an instant.
Time only moves forward.
So through time I must move too
day by day
or hour by hour,
but right now, only minute by minute.

I Bend at the Garden

The comb clutches the tangled mat of hair
at the back of my head.
I pull ever so slightly
and the whole mass releases from its moorings
painless.
A comb of golden red strands, hundreds, DNA, mine
ages old
now in the trash.
But then a thought—
I reach into the garbage can and
tread out the patio door and down the steps
the breeze chills my face
my mission ahead
the little white dog trotting softly behind.
At the edge of the flower bed
I bend and flip my head forward so the remaining hairs wave in the
     breeze
I cut blindly
with the scissors chopping until only a thin crop is left
dropping the strands into the soil
amidst the narcissus emerging from winter hibernation
and purple crocus in bud.
I let them waft upon the wind into the grass beyond
my DNA spread upon the garden.
I feel refreshed as if a new day has begun
and I am replenishing the Earth and my soul.

Physiology Experiment

I am part of an experiment
like a beagle in the vivarium
conditioned to lie on the table
for a weekly infusion
of a toxic medication.
I sit
arm outstretched
waiting for the prick of the needle.
I no longer watch
I just hope
my veins will last
long enough.
Only eight more rounds they say
but this is only the beginning.
There are more weeks to come
when the radiation begins
and once again I will lie down
breast dangling
exposed to the healing beam
or the killing beam
which ever it is.

Tail between My Legs

I feel like an old dog
after a long winter standing outside
where I grew a coat of thick, lush hair
to shield my rump from the icy wind and snow.
But now it is spring.
The sun is warm.
I pull the brush across my back and
collect a soft carpet of hair
falling around my paws.

Stranded

I embraced
the idea that my hair
would thin, but not fall,
until it did.
The strands covered
my pillow
in disarrayed piles of
copper, blonde and grey.
I thought I would be strong enough
and said it wouldn't matter—that I would shave it off
but when it began to fall
I wasn't
and I didn't.
Instead I put my hand on it
and ran my fingers through it
I coddled it and stroked it
thinking if I did that, it would last, but it didn't.

Friend

I am quiet
I tell few
It is more about me
than it is about you.
I don't want to discuss it
I don't want to share
I don't want to respond
Even if you care.

Risk Factor

No family history.
Never smoked cigarettes
or used illegal drugs
Not overweight.
Consuming
whole grains,
fruits,
vegetables
and little red meat.
Physically active
walking that dog
two miles each day
my 10,000 steps achieved.
Yet here I am
the girl with dense breasts
who had the regular mammograms and ultrasounds
for nearly 20 years.
Then at 3 a.m. that day
awakened by a subliminal force.
Some light
some energy unknown
that put my finger on a small
nondescript bump,
smooth and rounded
with all the features of 'benign'
but was not.

Silence

If you know me
and really care
you will hear me
in the silence
of today.

Walk with Me

I asked you to walk
with me
down the road.
A little exercise
for dog and me
and you.
But you said
No.
You were too busy
couldn't I see?
Enraptured by the computer
or news channel
or project *d'jour*.
I was just looking for time
together
to wander the road
and watch the hawks
and look for flowers
But you said no.
Should I remind you of my plight
or the thoughts whirring in my head
or
are you too busy for that as well?

Chemo-smiles

Chemotherapy seems an endless journey
but there are surprises
that no one mentions
consider it graveside humor
but maybe it's a chemo-smile moment.
Chemo-smiles occur
when I don't have to shave
my legs
or anything else
until months after the infusions end.
Then there is the grin
when I realize that no one
knows I'm wearing a wig.
People comment "Your hair is so shiny!" and
I think about the synthetic monofilament
and laugh to myself
because I am feeling so weak.
Chemo-smiles come
when those stubby nubbins near my eyes return as eyelashes,
after I learned to fake it with eyeliner and powder,
and then there is the day my head is covered with a furry baby hair.
With luck I will never be bald again. I will never have chemo again.
I will never have to return to the infusion room surrounded by those
other strong brave souls
enduring the journey in the chemo-club.

Solo Trip

I travel this path alone
into a dark unknown
not knowing the turns
or the dropoffs.
Other trips you take with friends
and children
and lovers
but this is a solitary journey
that will change my body
and may change my soul.
At first I fought
every step
but then I surrendered
to the pain, the hair loss
and the awkward glances
of those who wouldn't look at me.

Don't Ask

Let's talk, but don't ask me how I feel.
Don't tell me it wasn't so bad
or that the side effects were minimal
because the story is mine
you have no idea.
The truth is
the chemo was hell and
I hope IT is gone.
I am grateful for the care.
But I don't feel whole.
My energy is low
and I want to sleep.
My hair is merely stubble,
my nails are pitted and grey,
and my feet ache
because this story is mine.

Drowning

Engulfed in darkness
water all around
struggling to breathe,
the power of the wave
overwhelms
pulling and pushing
rolling and twisting
contorting my captive soul
tossing it skyward
and then churning me into the rocks.

Swimming

The journey began
with a first step
that took me into the depths
of an ocean so dark and lonely
that there were days
when I was uncertain
about everything.
I dove down
into the frigid water
amidst the others
swimming
for life
Swimming against the tide
scraping into the barnacles
and making it impossible
to pass without scars.

Markers

Hair and nails
indicators
of the journey.
Not that they were
beautiful
or special
or perfect
in any way
before.
But once they were presentable.
Then
they caught fire and burned
and the ice didn't help
and the hair fell out
and nail beds bled.

Battleground

Everyone suggested
I battle it
but
the rain was too heavy
and the lightening too fierce
I just couldn't cope
so
I surrendered my will
and my self
and my control
and then I survived.

New Things I

I am learning new things:
How to paint my nails
to hide the dead tissue and crusted hemorrhages
deep beneath my fingernails
all the ravages of chemotherapy.

New Things II

I am learning new things:
How to nap midday.
How to breathe in and out
slowly
following each expiration to its end.
How to put my mind
in another place
when the nurse puts the needle in my arm.

New Things III

I am learning new things:
How to use a crayon to draw in my missing eyebrows
How to put eyeliner on
in a weak attempt
to appear normal.
After all, everyone says
The eyes have it.

New Things IV

I am learning new things:
How cold
a
hairless
head
can be
in a gentle
summer breeze.

August 8th

Karen Loprete is gone.
Snatched.
We mourn
her funky style
her flower-power quilts
and Bohemian ways.
How am I still here?

Time Passes

What was it worth?
What did I gain?
Visual migraines,
dry skin,
scars,
and splintered nails
but also
the ability to see
the good and the evil
the truth and the lies
patience with time,
and place,
and people.

Good Will

I gave away the shoes
that hurt my feet, and
the sweaters
that were too tight.
I gave away the copper heels
and the chocolate brown lace
that I planned to wear
but never did.

All in the Art

Making saved me
even as I dangled at
the edge of the swamp.
It was the art and writing
that reminded me
of the joy,
of what was
and what is,
what is important,
and
what is not.

On Paper

Poems to express
what I cannot say.
Removed from my mind
and planted firmly on the paper
like Harry Potter and his wand
in the pensieve bowl
of thoughts.
Taking the memory,
the troubles,
the images,
out of my mind
and storing them until
I write
the next poem.

Holiday Letter

The year slipped away after January.
I was biopsied in February, followed with lumpectomy and sentinel node biopsy.
Then the chemo started and there was a needle in my vein
every Tuesday.
And then it was March.
My head and hands burned,
my hair fell out and my nail beds died.
After twelve Tuesdays they gave me a vacation.
"Rest up", they said.
We drove to Lake Erie. I walked. I paddled. I watched the eagles soar.
June 7th was our 30th anniversary.
That day I started daily radiation treatments.
I was tired. Dom cooked. I went to bed early.
The IV came every 3rd Tuesday for the next 9 months.
There were no fireworks July 4th.
The wig was still shiny but I was not.
By September I traveled in a baseball cap
and tried to ignore the people who stared
or looked away.
At the annual retreat in January
I was quiet.
Most of the quilters did not know the story.
Some didn't recognize me.
My hair was an odd pixie-puff.
I didn't explain.
I casually said I was tired of the salon expense,
But some of the women knew.
They had seen it before.
The look
in the eyes of friends
Some of whom were gone.
The questions ended and they hugged me.
And we sat and stitched,
laughed and sewed,
and thought of better days.

2yr 2mo 2d

Two years, two months, and two days
My husband and I open the summer cottage
Relieved that the pipes don't leak
when the water is turned on.
Neighbor Marge tells us how her friend Effie
is now gone.
And I think about being given at least
the last two years, two months, and two days.

Epilogue

Mary had a recurrence in 2018 and is currently in treatment.

Mary Lachman is a surgical pathologist, writer and visual artist. She grew up in Suffield, Ohio and graduated from The Ohio State University. She earned an M.D. from the University of Toledo Medical School and completed residency and fellowship training in pathology.

In addition to being the author of numerous scientific journal articles and several book chapters, Lachman has written about her art for *Quilting Arts Magazine* and *Quilting Arts Holiday*. Her debut publication, *Moth at the Window: Recollections of Indiana and Poetry of G. W. Clayton*, was published by Xlibris in 2014.

A self-taught visual artist working primarily in textiles, she has exhibited regionally and nationally. One of her art quilts is in the permanent collection at the Kresege Art Museum at Michigan State University. Another was selected for the cover of *The Healing Art of Pathology* published by the College of American Pathologists in 2016.

CPSIA information can be obtained
at www.ICGtesting.com
Printed in the USA
BVHW031406220819
556561BV00001B/224/P

9 781635 349863